Cool
Family Parties

Perfect Party Planning for Kids

Karen Latchana Kenney

A Division of ABDO

ABDO
Publishing Company

visit us at www.abdopublishing.com

Published by ABDO Publishing Company, a division of ABDO, P.O. Box 398166, Minneapolis, Minnesota 55439. Copyright © 2012 by Abdo Consulting Group, Inc. International copyrights reserved in all countries. No part of this book may be reproduced in any form without written permission from the publisher. Checkerboard Library™ is a trademark and logo of ABDO Publishing Company.

Printed in the United States of America, North Mankato, Minnesota
052011
092011

PRINTED ON RECYCLED PAPER

Interior Design and Production: Colleen Dolphin, Mighty Media, Inc.
Cover Design: Aaron DeYoe
Series Editor: Liz Salzmann
Photo Credits: Colleen Dolphin, Shutterstock

The following manufacturers/names appearing in this book are trademarks:
Elmer's® Glue-All®, Ferry-Morse® Seeds, FloraCraft® Floral Wire, Glue Dots® Adhesive Dots, National Home Gardening Club® Seeds, Office Depot® Poster Board, Oster® Osterizer Blender, Pyrex® Measuring Glass, Recollections® Photo Corners, Sharpie® Fine Point Marker

Library of Congress Cataloging-in-Publication Data

Kenney, Karen Latchana.
  Cool family parties : perfect party planning for kids / Karen Latchana Kenney.
      p. cm. -- (Cool parties)
  Includes index.
  ISBN 978-1-61714-973-3
  1. Children's parties--Planning--Juvenile literature. 2. Family recreation--Planning--Juvenile literature. I. Title. II. Series.

  GV1205.K456 2012
  793.2'1--dc22

2011003503

Contents

It's Family Party Time!.................................... 4

Party Planning Basics 6

What's Your Theme? 8

Tools & Supplies... 10

Invitations

Graduation Invitation 12

Decorations

Mother's Day Bouquet 14

Party Favors

Love Grows Seed Packet 16

Party Food

What's on the Menu? 18

Sample Party Menus 20

Tart and Sweet Strawberry Lemonade 22

Party Activities

Who's That Baby? 24

Duct Tape Wallet 26

Birthday Bingo 28

Conclusion... 30

Glossary 31

Web Sites... 31

Index.. 32

It's Family Party Time!

Getting together with family can be so fun! You celebrate birthdays and anniversaries together. You can meet distant relatives at reunions. And you can talk about old memories. Family parties are times to catch up and show your love for your family.

But to make this party happen, you need to plan out the **details**. Start with the basics, like the *when* and *where* of the party. Then move on to details like decorations and **menus**. Create some cool invitations and send them out. And don't forget to plan the activities! They keep the party moving at a fun pace.

Remember to plan and do as much as you can before the party starts. It takes time and hard work to be a host. But it's definitely worth it! Then all that's left for you to do is have fun!

Safety

- Ask for an adult's help when making food for your party.

- Find out where you can make crafts and play games. Do you need to protect a table surface? What should you use?

- Check the party room. Can anything be broken easily? Ask a parent to remove it before the party.

Permission

- Where in the house can you have the party? Are any rooms off-limits?

- How much money can you spend? Where can you shop and who will take you?

- Can you put up decorations? How?

- Who will help set up the party? Ask family members to do some of the tasks.

- Talk about who will clean up after the party.

Party Planning Basics

Every great party has the same basic **details**. They are the *who, what, when,* and *where* of the party. Your party planning should begin with these basics. Then make lists of everything you need to buy, make, and do for the party. You should also have a list of everyone you invited. Mark whether each guest can come or not.

Who: How many people do you want to invite? And who will they be?

What: What are you celebrating? You'll need to explain this on the invitation.

When: It's best to have a family party on a holiday or a weekend.

Where: Is the party at your house, at a park, or at a party room? Explain the details to your guests. And don't forget to include directions!

Favors:

What to buy:

What to make:

Activities:

What to buy:

What to make:

Menu:

Decorations:

What to buy:

What to make:

Music:

Equipment:

Guests:

_____ yes/no

_____ yes/no

_____ yes/no

_____ yes/no

_____ yes/no

_____ yes/no

7

What's Your Theme?

It's fun to have a theme for your party. A theme can be based on an idea or a **celebration**.

There are many themes to choose from. Pick one that fits your family. Then plan all the **details** around that theme. For example, you can make bug-shaped invitations for a family picnic. Or heart decorations for an anniversary party. Using a theme makes all the elements of your party go together. Check out the party themes on the next page. There are activities in this book to match each one.

Birthday

It's the day someone in your family was born! Funny hats and balloons make the party great. Don't forget the birthday cake!

Anniversary

Every year a couple celebrates the day they were married. Decorate with hearts and other **symbols** of love.

Family Picnic

Invite your family to a park. Eat lunch on a blanket. Then play games or go for a hike.

Reunion

When a group of family members get together, it's a reunion. Distant cousins and great-aunts show up. Make a lot of food that tastes great!

Mother's Day

This day is all about Mom. Bring her breakfast in bed. Give her flowers. And make her a very special card.

Father's Day

Show Dad how great he is on this day. Serve him a super lunch. Then do something together that is fun for both of you.

Graduation

Someone graduated from school! Invite family and friends over for a party. Use decorations shaped like **diplomas** or graduation caps.

Don't forget...

After you pick your theme, let guests know all about it. Do they need to bring something or wear special clothes? Let them know on the invitation. That way guests will show up prepared. They'll also be even more excited to party!

Tools & Supplies

Here are some of the things you'll need to do the activities in this book:

vase

bowl

zester

pitcher

blender

lemons

strawberries

saucepan

cutting board

juicer

knife

sparkling water

liquid measuring cup

measuring spoons

sugar

strainer

ribbon

hole punch

wire cutters

posterboard

rubber stamp

crepe paper, different colors

card stock, black & white

florist's wire

glue

adhesive dots

flower seeds

glassine envelopes

ink pad

markers

florist's tape

scissors

colored paper

duct tape, any color

photo corners, black

cutting mat

ruler

11

Graduation Invitation

This diploma invite helps get the word out!

What You Need

black card stock
white card stock
ruler
scissors
pencil
black photo corners
pen or markers
thin black ribbon
adhesive dots

You're Invited

TO JOIN IN CELEBRATING

What: JENNY'S GRADUATION

Where: 10 JUNIPER AVE.

When: JUNE 1

Jennifer Wilson

Please R.S.V.P. by May 25

12

Graduation Theme

 1 Cut out a 5 x 7-inch (13 x 18 cm) piece of black card stock. Then cut out a 4 x 6-inch (10 x 15 cm) piece of white card stock. Center the white card over the black card. Use a pencil to mark the corners on the black card.

 2 Remove the white card. Stick the photo corners onto the black card at the pencil marks.

 3 Write "You're Invited" in big letters across the top of the white card. Add the party **details** below it. Draw a line at the bottom of the card and sign it.

 4 Cut a 6-inch (15 cm) piece of black ribbon. Turn the black card over. Stick the end of the ribbon to the card with an adhesive dot. Put it 1½ inches (4 cm) from the right edge and 2 inches (5 cm) from the top.

5 Put an adhesive dot in the middle of the front of the black card. Put the white card in the photo corners. Flip the ribbon over the front of the card.

More Ideas!

PICNIC THEME
Make caterpillar invitations. Cut circles out of colored paper and connect them with brads. Write the party details on the circles. Then slide the circles together.

MOTHER'S DAY THEME
Cut little flowers out of card stock with a flower-shaped hole punch. Glue the flowers to a card and draw stems. It will look like a **bouquet**!

FATHER'S DAY THEME
Make a simple pop-up card. Find the instructions in *Cool International Parties*. Glue a picture of you and your dad on the pop-up section.

Mother's Day Bouquet

Your mom can enjoy these flowers forever!

What You Need

- crepe paper in different colors
- ruler
- scissors
- green florist's wire
- green florist's tape
- wire cutters
- vase

Mother's Day Theme

1 Choose two colors of crepe paper. Cut three strips of each. The strips should be 2½ x 4 inches (6 x 10 cm). Lay the three strips of one color on top of each other. Fold the long side of the strips up ¼ inch (.5 cm). Flip them over and fold again. Repeat until the strips are completely folded. Fold the other three strips together the same way.

2 Cut a V shape into each end of the folded strips. Then pinch the middle of each folded strip from the folded edges in.

3 Cut a 14-inch (36 cm) piece of florist's wire. Hold the two folded strips together. Wrap the end of the florist's wire around the middle of the strips. Then twist the end around the wire. Wrap florist's tape around the whole length of the wire to make the stem. Fluff out the ends of the crepe paper to make the flower.

4 Repeat steps 1 through 3 to make more flowers. Arrange the **bouquet** in a vase.

More Ideas!

GRADUATION THEME
Buy balloons in your school colors. Blow them up and tape them around a doorway. It makes a cool balloon arch!

PICNIC THEME
Place mats are great to use on picnic tables. Weave strips of colored paper together to make a mat. Put it between two pieces of contact paper. Trim the edges.

ANNIVERSARY THEME
Collect old and new pictures of the couple. Photocopy the pictures. Arrange them on posterboard. It will bring back wonderful memories!

Love Grows Seed Packet

Give flower seeds that will grow and thrive!

16

AnniversaryTheme

 1 Cut a piece of colored paper to fit in the envelope. Write the name of the plant and the planting instructions on it.

 2 Stamp a flower **design** onto the front of the envelope. Use a marker to write "Love Grows" on the envelope. Let the ink dry.

 3 Put the instructions and seeds in the envelope. Face the writing toward the back. Close the envelope. Punch two holes through the top of the envelope about ½ inch (1 cm) apart. The holes should go through the flap and the envelope.

 4 Cut a piece of ribbon 7½ inches (19 cm) long. Cut each end of the ribbon at an angle. Push one end of the ribbon through each hole from front to back. There should be the same amount of ribbon on each side of the holes.

 5 Flip the envelope over. Cross the ends of the ribbon. Push each end through the opposite hole from back to front. Pull the ends through.

More Ideas!

REUNION THEME
Create covers for small photo albums. Put your family's name and a family picture on the front. Set them out for family members to take home.

BIRTHDAY THEME
Decorate small tote bags with fabric markers. Add iron-on patches. Then fill them up with candy or small toys.

GRADUATION THEME
Make a bookmark from card stock. Write your graduation year on it. Add other designs. Punch a hole at the top. Tie a **tassel** through the hole.

What's on the Menu?

A great party isn't complete without delicious snacks and cool drinks! It's best to make finger foods. They are fun to eat and easy to carry. Everyone can still mingle while they snack. To plan your party **menu**, think about a few things first.

Variety

Everyone has different tastes. Make sure you have some sweet and some salty things. Have healthy choices and **vegetarian** dishes too.

Meals

Will your party last a long time? You will need more than just snacks if it does. Think about the time of day when your party will take place. Will your guests need breakfast, lunch, or dinner? And maybe they'll want snacks too!

Amount

How many people are coming? Plan to have enough food to feed everyone.

Time

It takes time to shop for and prepare food. Pick recipes that you have time to make. Remember, there are other things you need to do before the party.

Allergies

Check with your guests to see if they have any food **allergies**. Make sure there are things those guests can eat.

Sample Party Menus

It's fun to plan your menu around your party theme. Here are some examples.

Family Reunion Fiesta Menu

Guacamole and Tortilla Chips

Corn and Black Bean Salad

Pulled Pork Tacos

Tres Leches Cake (Three Milk Cake)

Mexican Sodas and Sparkling Water

Picture Perfect Picnic Menu

Tart & Sweet Lemonade*
*recipe on page 22!

Crispy Rice Bars

Hefty Hamburgers with Cheese

Creamy Potato Salad

Strawberry Shortcake

Garden Fresh Birthday Party Menu

Ants on a Log Celery Sticks

Dilly Dip and Crispy Potato Chips

Mini Pigs in a Blanket

Chocolate Cookie "Dirt" Sundaes

Pineapple Sparkler Punch

The Best Mother's Day Menu

Mango and Strawberry Fruit Cups

Spinach and Citrus Salad

Herbed Cheese Quiche

Lemon Cake

Peppermint Iced Tea

Ask for help finding easy and delicious recipes to make.

Tart & Sweet Lemonade

A refreshing drink for your next picnic!

What You Need

zester
bowl
6 lemons
measuring spoon
juicer
liquid measuring cup
2 cups plain water
1 cup sugar
saucepan
spoon
strainer
pitcher
1 pint strawberries
knife
cutting board
blender
2 cups sparkling water
ice

Picnic Theme

1. Make lemon **zest**. Scrape the zester over the skin of a lemon. Do not go deeper than the yellow part of the skin. You will need 1 tablespoon of lemon zest.

2. Juice the lemons using the juicer. Pour the juice into the measuring cup. You will need 1 cup of lemon juice. Make sure to keep the seeds out!

3. Put the plain water and sugar in a saucepan. Bring it to a boil. Then lower the heat to a simmer. Keep cooking and stirring until the sugar **dissolves**.

4. Stir in the lemon juice and zest. Remove the pan from the heat. Let the mixture cool and then strain it into a pitcher.

5. Wash the strawberries and cut them in half. Remove the stems and the white part in the middle. **Purée** the strawberries in the blender.

6. Add the puréed strawberries to the pitcher. Put it in the refrigerator until chilled.

7. To serve, add the sparkling water to the pitcher. Pour the lemonade into glasses of ice.

Who's That Baby?

See who still looks like their baby picture!

What You Need

copies of baby pictures
posterboard
markers
glue
paper
pen

WHO'S THAT BABY?

I am a doctor with three nieces and four nephews.

1

I have two dogs and golf every Saturday.

2

I have three children and ten grandchildren.

3

pizza and am

24

Reunion Theme

1 Before the reunion, collect baby pictures of each family member. Think of clues for each person, such as, "I have two brothers and my mom has red hair."

2 Write "Who's That Baby?" in big letters at the top of the posterboard.

3 Glue the pictures to the posterboard in rows. Write the clues below the pictures. Number each picture.

4 Make a form for guests to use for their guesses. Write "Who's That Baby? Answers" at the top. Then list the numbers of the pictures and draw answer lines. Make a copy for each guest. Make an answer key so you can check everyone's guesses.

5 At the reunion, set the board where everyone can see it. Tell guests to guess which adult matches each baby picture. Give prizes to the people who get the most answers right.

More Ideas!

ANNIVERSARY THEME
What do you know about the couple? Write trivia questions on cards. Set them out so guests can guess the answers.

PICNIC THEME
It's fun to have three-legged races at a picnic. Have everyone find a partner. Each pair ties two of their legs together. Then everyone tries to run the race!

MOTHER'S DAY THEME
Moms love handmade beaded bracelets. Use bead colors that she likes. Add charms that remind you of your mom.

Duct Tape Wallet

You can use duct tape for almost anything!

Father's Day Theme

1 Cut a piece of tape 7 inches (18 cm) long. Lay it on the mat with the sticky side up. Cut another piece of tape. Stick it to the first piece with the long sides overlapping slightly. Add two more pieces of tape. You will have a sheet of duct tape.

2 Cut a piece of tape 4 inches (10 cm) long. Lay it sticky side down crosswise along one end of the sheet. Cut another piece of tape. Lay it down so it overlaps the first piece. Continue to add tape until the sheet is covered.

3 Trim the edges straight. Fold the sheet lengthwise. Cut a 4-inch (10 cm) piece of tape. Put it over one of the short ends. Trim off the extra tape.

4 Fold the **wallet** crosswise. If the open end is uneven, trim it straight. Cover the open short end with a 4-inch (10 cm) piece of tape. Trim off the extra tape.

More Ideas!

ANNIVERSARY THEME
Make a memory scrapbook. Put a picture from the couple's wedding on the cover. Then ask each guest to write a memory of the couple in the book.

FATHER'S DAY THEME
Paint a wooden frame with your dad's favorite colors. Then write a message to your dad around the frame. Put a picture of you and your dad in the frame.

GRADUATION THEME
Make a "yearbook" T-shirt. Set out a plain white shirt and fabric markers. Put a piece of cardboard in the shirt to keep it flat. Ask everyone to sign the shirt.

Birthday Bingo

What You Need

computer and printer
 (or use paper and markers)

paper

scissors

markers

bowl

prizes (optional)

A game of luck that everyone can play!

28

Birthday Theme

Birthday Bingo Word List

Birthday Bingo Word List
cake
hat
party
candle
game
present
gift
surprise
wrapp
prize

Birthday Bingo

FREE

1 Make a list of as many birthday-related words as you can. You should have at least 30 words. Leave enough room to cut around the words. Make a bingo card. Create a **grid** with five boxes across and five boxes down. Put FREE in the center box. Add some decorations above the grid.

2 Print out the birthday words sheet. Cut the words apart and put them in a bowl. Print a copy of the word list and the bingo card for each guest.

3 At the party, have the guests write a word from the list in each box on their cards. Each box has to have a different word.

4 The bingo caller picks a word out of the bowl. Anyone who has that word on their card draws an X over it. Then the caller picks another word.

5 The first person to cross out a row of words shouts "Bingo!" and wins the game! The row can be across, up-and-down, or diagonal.

More Ideas!

REUNION THEME
Draw a family tree on a large sheet of paper. Add the two sets of grandparents at the top. Then ask family members to fill in their spots on the tree.

BIRTHDAY THEME
Make birthday crowns out of posterboard. Cut strips with points on one side. Decorate them with gems and markers. Tape the ends together.

FATHER'S DAY THEME
If your dad likes to cook on the grill, make him an apron! Just decorate a plain apron using fabric markers. Add a funny saying.

Conclusion

Did you have a great time with your family? Getting together with family makes special memories. But, the party room is a mess! There's still work to do. Make sure you clean up and put everything back in order. Your family will thank you for your help.

Was it someone's birthday? Did you keep track of who brought which gifts? It's important to write down who gave what. That will make it easier for the birthday person to send thank-you cards. Make thank-you cards that match the party's theme. Write something **unique** and personal on each guest's card. Then send out the cards within a week after the party.

Hosting a party is hard work! There are so many **details** to plan and things to make. In the end, though, it all comes together to make a party to remember. Family parties are fun, but what will your next party be? Check out the other books in the *Cool Parties* series for more great ideas.

Glossary

allergy – sickness caused by touching, breathing, or eating certain things.

bouquet – a bunch of flowers gathered together or arranged in a vase.

celebration – a party or festival held to mark a special occasion.

design – a decorative pattern or arrangement.

detail – a small part of something.

diploma – a document that states that a student has finished school.

dissolve – to mix with a liquid so that it becomes part of the liquid.

grid – a pattern with rows of squares, such as a checkerboard.

menu – a list of things to choose from.

purée – to make very smooth and creamy using a blender.

symbol – an object or picture that stands for or represents something.

tassel – a string with a fluffy end that is tied to something for decoration.

unique – different, unusual, or special.

vegetarian – without any meat.

wallet – a flat case to keep money or pictures in.

zest – a small piece of the peel of a citrus fruit, such as a lemon, lime, or orange. A *zester* is a tool used to scrape citrus peels.

Web Sites

To learn more about cool parties, visit ABDO Publishing Company on the World Wide Web at **www.abdopublishing.com**. Web sites about cool parties are featured on our book links page. These links are routinely monitored and updated to provide the most current information available.

Index

A

Activities and crafts
  doing, 24–25, 26–27, 28–29
  planning, 4, 5, 8–9
Adult help, for safety, 5
Allergies, to foods, 19
Anniversary theme party,
  9, 15, 16–17, 25, 27

B

Basic details, planning,
  4, 5, 6–7
Birthday theme party,
  9, 17, 21, 28–29

C

Cleaning up, 5, 30
Cost, 5

D

Decorations
  making, 14–15
  planning, 4, 5, 8–9

F

Father's Day theme party,
  9, 13, 26–27, 29
Favors
  making, 16–17
  planning, 8–9

Food

Food
  planning, 4, 18–19
  recipes, 22–23
  sample menus, 20–21

G

Graduation theme party,
  9, 12–13, 15, 17, 27
Guest list, 6, 7
Guests, responsibilities of, 9

H

Hosts, responsibilities of, 4, 30

I

Invitations
  making, 12–13
  planning, 4, 9

L

Lemonade, recipe for, 22–23
Lists, for planning, 6–7

M

Menu
  planning, 4, 18–19
  samples, 20–21
Mother's Day theme party,
  9, 13, 14–15, 21, 25

P

Permission, for planning and
  hosting, 5
Picnic theme party,
  9, 13, 15, 20, 22–23, 25

R

Reunion theme party,
  9, 17, 20, 24–25, 29

S

Safety, 5

T

Thank-you cards, 30
Themes, choosing and planning,
  4, 6, 8–9
Tools and supplies, 10–11